String Techniques
for
Superior Musical Performance
Robert S. Frost

Dear String Student,

Striving for superior performances is a worthy, appropriate, and obtainable goal. There are many skills that contribute to superior performance. Basic skills include the ability to play with good intonation in many keys, with correct rhythm, with a good tone, with a wide dynamic range and with correct articulation. Collectively, these skills determine one's musicianship.

String Techniques for Superior Musical Performance is designed to help you further develop and improve your musicianship leading to superior performances. The exercises, scales, chorales, etudes, and songs have been carefully selected to assist you. They are proven techniques that will help you become an outstanding musician. The order and flexibility of the materials allows you to focus on the skills you need most. They can be fun as well as challenging. Challenge your left hand with the **Finger Dexterity** exercises and etudes, your right hand with bowings and articulations, and your heart with musical performances.

Best wishes,

Robert S. Frost

ISBN 0-8497-3473-8

Section I: Technique, Tone, Tuning
Finger Dexterity

The word "dexterity" means agility or skill when using the hands. These exercises cover a multitude of left hand finger combinations using various patterns and rhythms so that left hand technique can strengthen. For full benefit, each example and exercise should be played using the key signatures shown directly below.

Key Signatures

| Example 1 | **Finger Runners** |

| Example 2 | **Rhythm Runners in $\frac{3}{4}$** |

The following Note Patterns can be played in a variety of ways and in various combinations:
1) Use each of the key signatures located above the Finger Runners.
2) Repeat each 2-bar segment (a.-h.) four times.
3) Use the Rhythm Runners (in $\frac{3}{4}$ time) when playing the note pattern segments.
4) Play on other strings.

1. Three-Note Patterns in $\frac{3}{4}$ Time

2. Four-Note Patterns in $\frac{3}{4}$ Time

3. Five-Note Patterns in $\frac{3}{4}$ Time

Play each scale four times as written. Add in slurs; try combinations of 2, 4, 8 notes per bow. Incorporate the complete ascending and descending scale as shown below.

4. Tetrachords in Scales

4a. Tetrachord Scale Pattern

Example 3 Finger Runners in 4/4

Example 4 Rhythm Runners in 4/4

a.

b.

Play the exercises found in #5, #6, and #7 using the key signatures found on page 2. Repeat each exercise 4 times; then, play using **Finger Runners in 4/4** for each exercise and in each key. Once finger patterns have been firmly established, play on other strings. Also, play using **Rhythm Runners** found on the Inside Front Cover.

5. Three-Note Patterns in 4/4 Time

a.   b.   c.   d.

e.   f.   g.   h.

6. Four-Note Patterns in 4/4 Time

a.   b.   c.

d.   e.

f.   g.   h.

7. Five-Note Patterns in 4/4 Time

> Play the ascending and descending versions with a détaché bow stroke. Once the left hand is comfortable, incorporate various slurring combinations. Also play using the key signatures found on page 2.

8. Running the Scale-Ascending

9. Running the Scale-Descending

Chromatics

Chromatic exercises are the natural next step after each tetrachord pattern has been learned. They should be practiced using **Finger Runners** and **Rhythm Runners**. Once the chromatic sequences are learned, they should be practiced on other strings.

Example 5 **Chromatic Fingerings**

Example 6 **Chromatic Finger Runners**

Example 7 **Rhythm Runners in $\frac{3}{4}$**

Repeat each segment 4 times; then play using **Finger Runners** and **Rhythm Runners** for each exercise. Once Chromatic Patterns have been further established, play on other strings.

10. Chromatic Patterns in $\frac{3}{4}$ Time

Play as written and using the bowing variations below.

11. Chromatic Etude #1

Nicolas Laoureux (b. 1863)

Bowing Variations:

12. Song of India

Nicolai Rimsky-Korsakov (1844-1908)

Example 8

Finger Runners in 4/4

Example 9

Rhythm Runners in 4/4

a.

b.

* = Round Entrance

Repeat each exercise 4 times, then play using **Finger Runners** and **Rhythm Runners** for each exercise. Once Chromatic Patterns have been firmly established, play on other strings.

13. Chromatic Patterns in 4/4 Time

a.   b.   c.

d.   e.   f.

g.   h.   i.

j.   k.   l.

14. D Chromatic Scale

15. Habañera

Georges Bizet (1838-1875)

Play as written; then in slurring combinations of two or four notes per bow, or slurring one bow per measure.

16. C and G Chromatic Scales

Practice both bowing options.

17. Chromatic Etude #2

Franz Wohlfahrt (1833-1884)
Op. 74, no. 25

Development and Control of Tone

18. Dynamic Options in ¾ Time

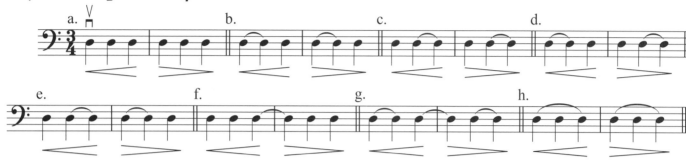

Practice as written with slow, even, sustained tones. Integrate piano, mezzo forte, and forte dynamics.

19. Tetrachord in D in ¾ Time

Practice #20 and #21 as written then apply **Dynamic Options in ¾** to each measure or to every two measures.

20. Tetrachord in G in ¾ Time

Practice the scale ascending and descending. Also play alternating dynamics by measure for example start measure 1 forte, then measure 2 piano, and so on.

21. C Scale Using Dynamics in ¾ Time

22. Dynamic Etude #1

Franz Wohlfahrt (1833-1884)

Op. 45, no. 8

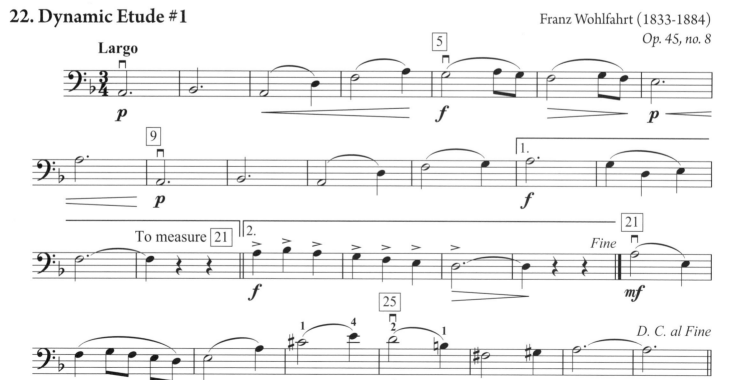

23. Dynamic Options in $\frac{4}{4}$ Time

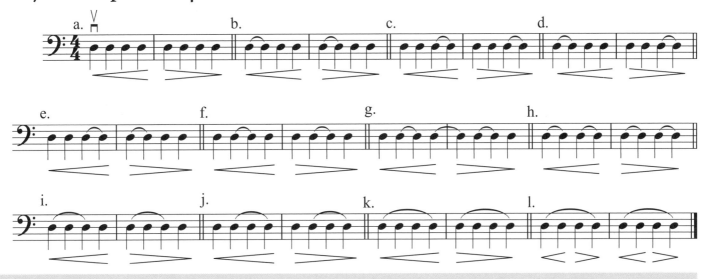

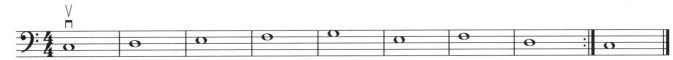

Practice as written using slow, even, sustained tones. Integrate piano, mezzo forte, and forte dynamics.

24. Tetrachord in C in $\frac{4}{4}$ Time

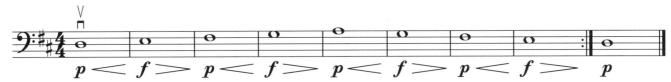

Practice #25 and #26 as written, then apply **Dynamic Options in $\frac{4}{4}$** to each measure or to every two measures.

25. Tetrachord in D in $\frac{4}{4}$ Time

Practice the scale ascending and descending. Also play alternating dynamics by measure for example start measure 1 forte, then measure 2 piano, and so on.

26. F Scale Using Dynamics in $\frac{4}{4}$ Time

27. Dynamic Etude #2

Josef Werner (1837-1922)

Op. 12, no. 3

Tuning

Play Part A or Part B as assigned. Practice slowly: tune the 2nd, then the unison, then the next 2nd, and so on.

28. Tuning Intervals – Unisons & 2nds

Use the previous exercise as a guide, practice each (interval) exercise: a. through f.

29. Tuning Intervals – 2nds & 3rds, 3rds & 4ths, etc.

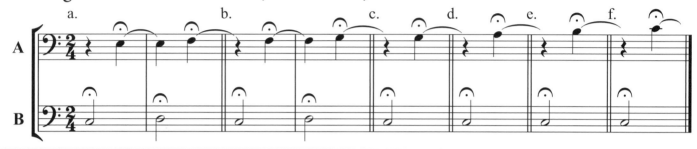

Use slow, sustained bows on Part B, bowing freely.

30. Tuning Intervals –Using a Drone

Play Part A or Part B as assigned. Practice slowly, using even, sustained bows. Hold and tune individual notes in Part A as necessary. Once the notes of the chords are well in tune, play #32. Apply concepts in this exercise to scales in Section II: Major and Minor Keys.

31. Building Chords on Scale Tones

When playing chords on scale tones, pay close attention to the whole steps and half steps dictated by the key signature. Practice slowly. Follow the voicing to complete the scale chords in segments b. and c. Play the scales ascending and descending. Also apply chord sequences to scales found in Section II.

32. Tuning Chords on Scale Tones

Use even, sustained bows when tuning individual chord tones. Hold individual parts until all chord tones are in tune. Once all chords have been tuned, play the chord progression without rests (end of measures 2, 4, 6, 8).

33. Tuning Chord Progressions

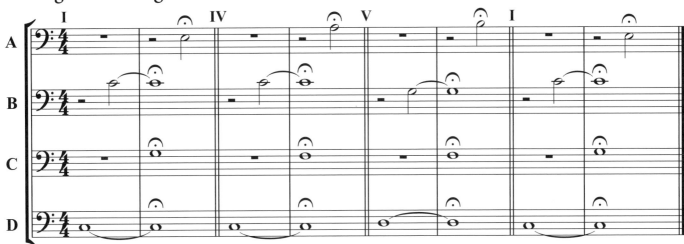

34. Sarabanda from Chamber Sonata III

Arcangelo Corelli (1653-1713)

Op. 4

Less Bows

Section II: Major and Minor Scales
C Major

Play #35, #36, and #37 as written and using bowings selected from the Appendix (pages 45-47).

35. C Major Scale

36. C Major Arpeggios

37. C Major Scale Etude

All Fingers down

38. Chorale

Johann Hermann Schein (1586-1630)

Play as written and using the bowings below. For variety, also play tremolo, measured or unmeasured.

39. C Major Etude

Franz Wohlfahrt (1833-1884)
Op. 45, no. 15

40. Romance in G

Ludwig van Beethoven (1770-1827)
Op. 40

G Major

Play #41, #42, and #43 as written and using bowings selected from the Appendix.

41. G Major Scale

42. G Major Arpeggios

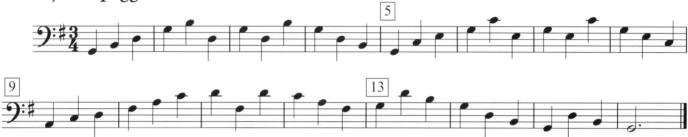

43. G Major Scale Etude

44. Chorale

Johann Sebastian Bach (1685-1750)

Play as written and using the bowings below.

45. G Major Etude

Richard Hofmann (1819-1909)
Op. 86, no. 5

46. Pavane for a Dead Princess

Maurice Ravel (1875-1937)

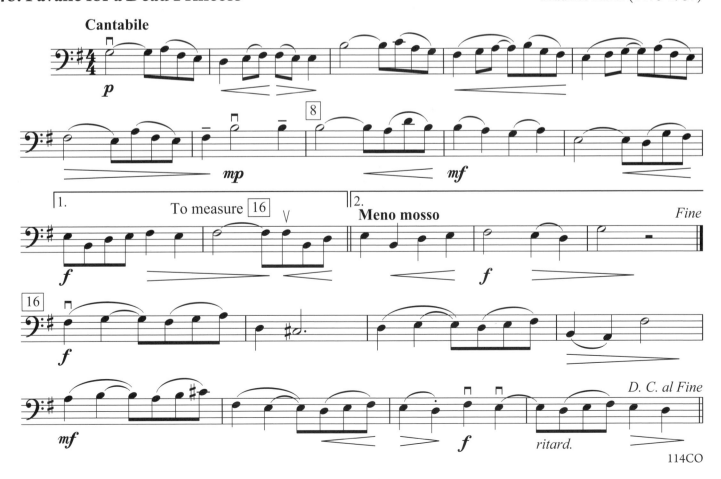

D Major

Play #47, #48, and #49 as written and using bowings found in the Appendix.

47. D Major Scale

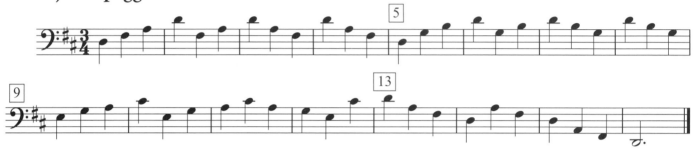

48. D Major Arpeggios

49. D Major Scale Etude

50. Chorale

Johann Gottfried Schicht (1753-1823)

Play as written and use the three bowing variations provided. For variety, also play pizzicato.

51. D Major Etude

Josef Werner (1837-1922)
Op. 12

5

9

13

17

Bowing Variations:

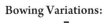

52. Procession of the Sardar (from "Caucasian Sketches")

M. M. Ippolitov-Ivanov (1859-1935)
Op. 10

A Major

Play #53, #54, and #55 as written and using bowings found in the Appendix.

53. A Major Scale

54. A Major Arpeggios

55. A Major Scale Etude

56. Chorale

Johann Sebastian Bach (1685-1750)

Play as written and using the three bowing variations provided. For variety, try playing with measured or unmeasured tremolo.

57. A Major Etude

Heinrich Ernst Kayser (1815-1888)
Op. 20, no. 5

Bowing Variations:

58. Theme – Pilgrims' Chorus (from "Tannhauser")

Richard Wagner (1813-1883)

Andante maestoso

F Major

Play #59, #60, and #61 as written and using bowings found in the Appendix.

59. F Major Scale

60. F Major Arpeggios

61. F Major Scale Etude

62. Chorale

Johann Sebastian Bach (1685-1750)

Play as written and use the three bowing variations provided.

63. F Major Etude

Franz Wohlfahrt (1833-1884)
Op. 54, no. 1

64. Theme – Scheherazade

Nicolai Rimsky-Korsakov (1844-1908)
Op. 35

Allegro moderato

Meno mosso

B♭ Major

Play #65, #66, and #67 as written and using bowings found in the Appendix.

65. B♭ Major Scale

66. B♭ Major Arpeggios

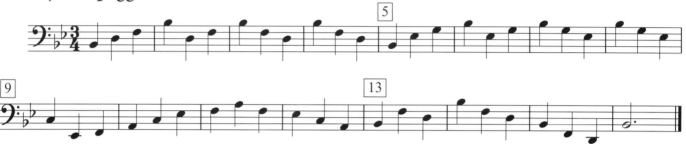

67. B♭ Major Scale Etude

68. Chorale

Johann Sebastian Bach (1685-1750)

Play as written and use the three bowing variations provided. For variety, also play pizzicato.

69. B♭ Major Etude

Franz Wohlfahrt (1833-1884)
Op. 45, no. 7

Bowing Variations:

70. Reverie

Claude Debussy (1862-1918)

E♭ Major

Play #71, #72, and #73 as written and using bowings found in the Appendix.

71. E♭ Major Scale

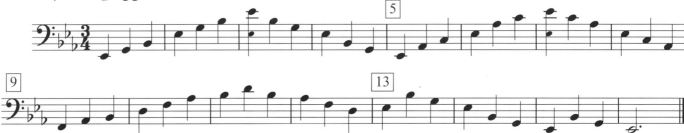

72. E♭ Major Arpeggios

73. E♭ Major Scale Etude

74. Chorale

Johann Schop (1590-1667)

Play as written and use the three bowing variations provided.

75. E♭ Major Etude

Richard Hofmann (1831-1909)
Op. 86, no. 16

76. Londonderry Air

Irish Folk Song

A Minor

Play #77, #78, and #79 as written and using bowings found in the Appendix.

77. A Minor Scale

78. A Minor Arpeggios

79. A Minor Scale Etude

80. Chorale

Georg Neumark (1621-1681)

Play as written and using the three bowing variations provided. For variety, play using dotted values. See the Appendix for suggestions.

81. A Minor Etude

Christian Heinrich Hohmann (1811-1861)

82. Theme – Symphony in D Minor

César Franck (1822-1880)

E Minor

Play #83, #84, and #85 as written and using bowings found in the Appendix.

83. E Minor Scale

84. E Minor Arpeggios

85. E Minor Scale Etude

86. Chorale

Johann Sebastian Bach (1685-1750)

Play as written and use the three bowing variations provided. For variety, also play pizzicato.

87. E Minor Etude

Justus Johann Friedrich Dotzauer (1783-1860)

Bowing Variations:

88. Theme – Symphony No. 9 (From The New World)

Antonín Dvořák (1841-1904)

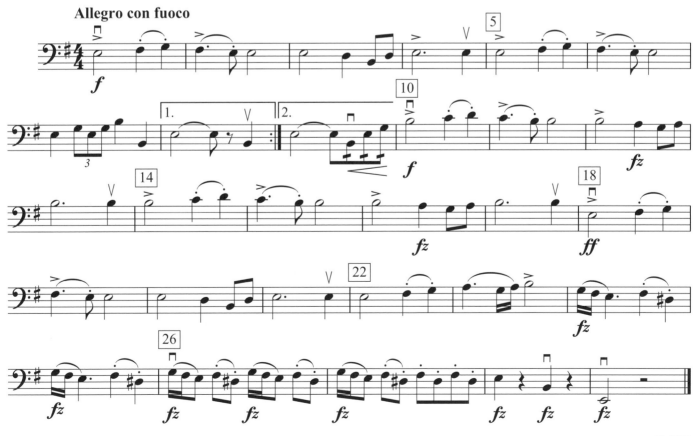

B Minor

Play #89, #90, and #91 as written and using bowings found in the Appendix.

89. B Minor Scale

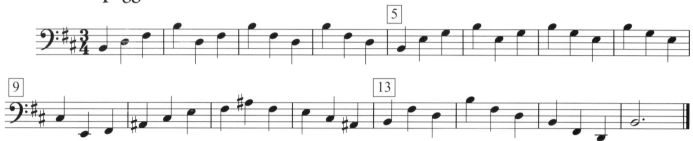

90. B Minor Arpeggios

91. B Minor Scale Etude

92. Chorale

Johann Sebastian Bach (1685-1750)

Play as written and use the three bowing variations provided. For variety, play measured tremolo, two notes per bow.

93. B Minor Etude

Hubert Leonard (1819-1890)

94. Theme – In the Hall of the Mountain King

Edvard Grieg (1843-1907)

34

D Minor

Play #95, #96, and #97 as written and using bowings found in the Appendix.

95. D Minor Scale

96. D Minor Arpeggios

97. D Minor Scale Etude

98. Chorale

Johann Sebastian Bach (1685-1750)

Play as written and use the three bowing variations provided.

99. D Minor Etude

Hans Sitt (1850-1922)
Op. 32, no. 20

100. Theme – Swan Lake

Peter Ilyich Tchaikovsky (1840-1893)

G Minor

Play #101, #102, and #103 as written and using bowings found in the Appendix.

101. G Minor Scale

102. G Minor Arpeggios

103. G Minor Scale Etude

104. Chorale

Johann Sebastian Bach (1685-1750)

Play as written and use the three bowing variations provided.

105. G Minor Etude

Christian Heinrich Hohmann (1811-1861)

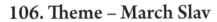

Bowing Variations:

106. Theme – March Slav

Peter Ilyich Tchaikovsky (1840-1893)

Op. 31

C Minor

Play #107, #108, and #109 as written and using bowings found in the Appendix.

107. C Minor Scale

108. C Minor Arpeggios

109. C Minor Scale Etude

110. Chorale

Heinrich Albert (1604-1651)

Play as written and use the three bowing and rhythm variations provided. For variety, also play pizzicato.

111. C Minor Etude

Richard Hofmann (1831-1909)
Op. 86, no. 2

112. Theme – Farandole from L'Arlésienne Suite No. 2

Georges Bizet (1838-1875)

Section III: Etudes & Bowing Styles
Spiccato & Sautillé

Begin practicing with bowing a., then progress to b. and c. and finally as written. Once a fast tempo is achieved, play again using sautillé; two or four bows per note.

113. Spiccato & Sautillé Etude #1

Sebastian Lee (1805-1887)

Bowing Variations:

Practice as written, spiccato, and using single bows at various tempos. Also play sautillé at a fast tempo using two or four bows per note.

114. Spiccato & Sautillé Etude #2

Nicolas Laoureux (b. 1863)

Practice as written, spiccato, and using single bows at various tempos. Also play sautillé at a fast tempo using two or four bows per note.

115. Spiccato & Sautillé Etude #3

Heinrich Ernst Kayser (1815-1888)

Op. 20, no. 1

Martelé

Practice as written using the middle of the bow. Practice each bowing below using long bows on slurred notes and short bows on separate martelé bows. See the Appendix for additional bowings.

116. Martelé Etude #1

Justus Johann Friedrich Dotzauer (1783-1860)

Bowing Variations:

Play as written and using separate bows. When playing as written, use bow division and maintain extra weight at the tip to produce a good martelé sound.

117. Martelé Etude #2

Jacques-Féréol Mazas (1782-1849)
Op. 36, no. 28

Play as written and using separate bows. See the Appendix for additional bowings.

118. Martelé Etude #3

Franz Wohlfahrt (1833-1884)
Op. 45, no. 11

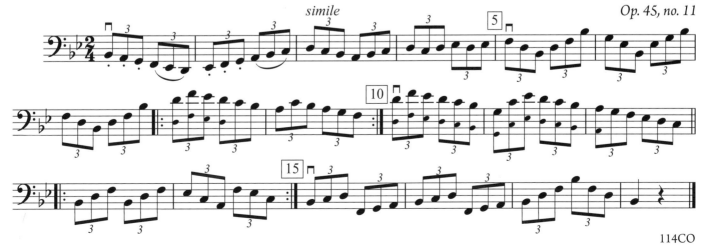

114CO

Staccato

Practice separate bows first; then, as written at various tempos and using various amounts of bow. Also use the three bowing variations provided.

119. Staccato Etude #1

Justus Johann Friedrich Dotzauer (1783-1860)

Bowing Variations:

Play as written and using separate bows. All notes should be played martelé.

120. Staccato Etude #2

Hans Sitt (1850-1922)

Op. 32, no. 9

Keep the bow firmly placed into the string to begin the up bow staccato. Use a fast down bow so that the staccato up bows begin in the upper bow.

121. Staccato Etude #3

Christian Heinrich Hohmann (1811-1861)

Portato

Practice as written and using each bowing below. When playing as written and with bowing a., use equal amounts of bow for each slur and especially an equal amount of bow for each portato note.

122. Portato Etude #1

Rodolphe Kreutzer (1766-1831)

Op. 2

Bowing Variations:

Refer to the Appendix for additional portato bowings.

123. Portato Etude #2

Richard Hofmann (1831-1909)

Op. 86, no. 8

124. Portato Etude #3

Franz Wohlfahrt (1833-1884)

Op. 45, no. 34

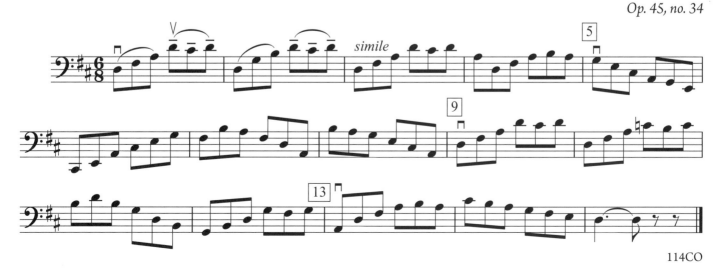

General Etudes

The two etudes in this section are suitable for practicing all bowings introduced in *String Techniques for Superior Musical Performance*: Détaché, Slurs, Martelé, Staccato, Spiccato, Sautillé, and Tremolo. Use the Appendix as a resource. As appropriate, play selected bowings at various tempos. Remember, pizzicato is also an important technique to develop tone. Again, using the Appendix as a resource, incorporate dotted rhythms to these etudes.

125. General Etude #1

Otakar Ševčík (1852-1934)
Op. 2, no. 7

126. General Etude #2

Otakar Ševčík (1852-1934)
Op. 2, no. 6

Appendix
Bowings and Articulations

Use the bowings and articulations in this Appendix to further develop bowing technique on scales, arpeggios, and etudes found in Sections II and III.

Note: The wide variety of bowings suggests that different tempos should be used for practice and performance, along with where the stroke is to be played on the bow, and the amount of bow used. Receive guidance regarding proper tempo and bow usage. Also remember that bow division and bow speed are important components to playing bowings properly and effectively.

C or 4/4

Détaché & Slurs	Martelé	Staccato	Louré or Portato
1.	13.	22.	31.
2.	14.	23.	32.
3.	15.	24.	33.
4.	16.	25.	34.
5.	17.	26.	35.
6.	18.	27.	36.
7.	19.	28.	37.
8.	20.	29.	38.
9.	21.	30.	
10.			
11.			
12.			

Bowings and Articulations

$$\frac{3}{4}$$

Détaché & Slurs	Martelé	Staccato	Louré or Portato

Bowings and Articulations

C or **4/4**

Spiccato & Sautillé

Tremolo

Measured

90.

Unmeasured

91.

Dotted Rhythms

6/8

Dotted Rhythms

Syncopation

C or **4/4**

99.

100.

3/4

101.

102.